SCIENCE SKILLS SORTED

HUMAN AND ANIMAL
BODIES

ANGELA ROYSTON

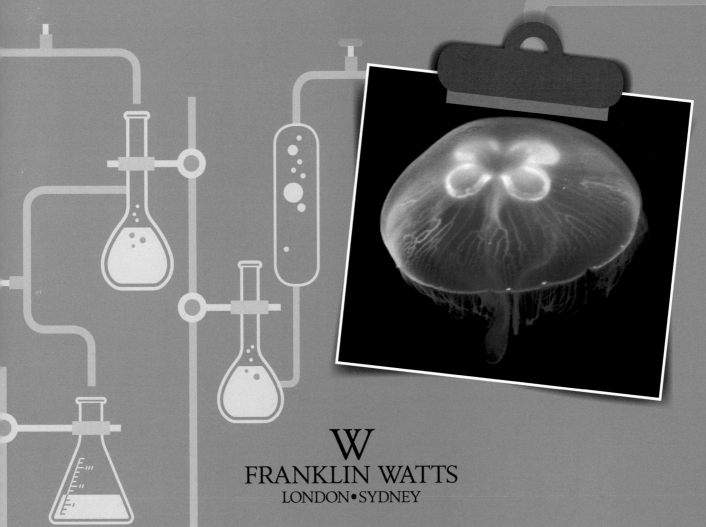

W

FRANKLIN WATTS
LONDON • SYDNEY

Franklin Watts
First published in Great Britain in 2017 by The Watts Publishing Group

Credits
Series Editor: Amy Pimperton
Series Designer: Emma DeBanks
Picture Researcher: Diana Morris
Picture credits: Ammit/Dreamstime: 16t. Anyaivanova/Dreamstime: 6t. Big Tuba online/Shutterstock: 20t. bikeriderlondon/Shutterstock: 17t. Blue Ring Media/Dreamstime: 5t. Williyam Bradbury/ Shutterstock: 14c. Barry Brown/Alamy: 18c. Wim Claes/Dreamstime: 16b. Paul Crash/Shutterstock: 3bc. Brett Crichley/Dreamstime: 15b. Designua/Shutterstock: 25t. Doethion/Dreamstime: 10c. D100/Shutterstock: 17cr. Srdjan Draskovic/Dreamstime: 4t. Ekrystia/Dreamstime: 12br. Michael & Patricia Fogden/Minden/FLPA Images: 3br, 10bl. Franz12/Shutterstock: 27b. Fraud/SPL: 20b. Natalia Garmasheva/Shutterstock: 22b. Vladimir Gjorgiev/Shutterstock: 19t. Gilbert S Grant /SPL: 12c. Gunita/ Dreamstime: 8t. Paul Hakimata/Dreamstime: 7b. Jubal Harshaw/Shutterstock: 9br. Ramona Heim/ Shutterstock: 26bl. Chris Howey/Dreamstime: 4b. Alexandr Iurochkin/Shutterstock: 20c. Jevtic/ Dreamstime: 22c. Julius/Shutterstock: 29b. Valeriy Kirsanov/Dreamstime: 12bl. Kateryna Kon/ Shutterstock: 21b. kpzfoto/Alamy: 26br. Lesscholz /Dreamstime: 12t. Timothy Craig Lubke/Shutterstock: 24t. Alina Maksimova/Dreamstime: 26cr. Sarah Marchant/Dreamstime: 21t. Martin Mark/Dreamstime: 6c. David Massaroni /Dreamstime: 5cr. Lipowski Milan/Shutterstock: 17b. Tony Mills/Shutterstock: 14b. Alex Mit/Shutterstock: 24c. MSSA/Shutterstock: 17cl. National Institutes of Health/SPL: 6b. Chris Newbert/Minden/FLPA Images: 24b. Nyvit-art/Shutterstock: 9bc. Oyls/Shutterstock: 22t. Ra3m/ Dreamstime: 15t. Helene Rogers/Art Directors and Trip/Alamy: 11b. Natalya Rozhkova/Shutterstock: 26t. Shahjehan/Shutterstock: 10t. Andrei Shumskiy/Shutterstock: 7r. StockPhotoAstur/Shutterstock: 23t. studio on line/Shutterstock: 11t. Spencer Sutton/SPL: 8b. Tim Heusinger Von Waldegge/Dreamstime: 1, 5cl. Heijo Van De Werf /Dreamstime: 10cr. Wikimedia Commons: 18b. Winfried Wisniewski/Getty Images: front cover. Alexander Y/Shutterstock: 8c. Jelina Zaric/Alamy: 26c. Abeselom Zerit/Shutterstock: 5br. Zachary Zirlin/Shutterstock: 19t.

HB ISBN 978 1 4451 5153 3
PB ISBN 978 1 4451 5154 0

Printed in China

Franklin Watts
An imprint of
Hachette Children's Group
Part of The Watts Publishing Group
Carmelite House
50 Victoria Embankment
London EC4Y 0DZ

An Hachette UK Company
www.hachette.co.uk

www.franklinwatts.co.uk

MIX
Paper from
responsible sources
FSC® C104740
www.fsc.org

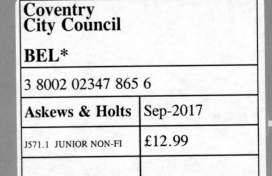

CONTENTS

Words in **bold** can be found in the glossary on page 30.

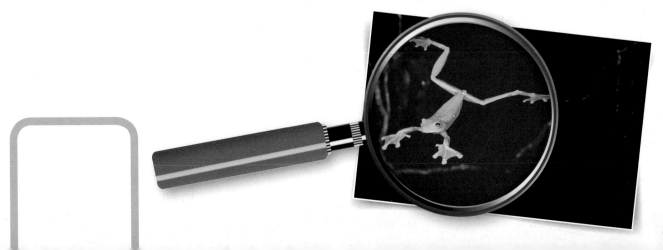

HUMANS AND OTHER ANIMALS

Living things are divided into large groups or kingdoms. Humans and other animals belong to the group called the animal kingdom. All living things share the same **life processes**: sensing their **environment**, movement, nutrition (feeding), respiration (breathing), excretion (getting rid of waste), growth, and reproduction (having young). What makes animals different is that they are the only living things that can move from one place to another under their own power.

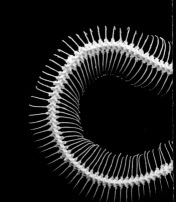

MOVING

Animals move for several reasons, including finding food, finding a mate and escaping from danger. Some animals move through water, others fly through the air, while many move in different ways across or under the ground. How they move depends on how their bodies are structured.

Kangaroos move by jumping, using their tail and long, powerful back legs.

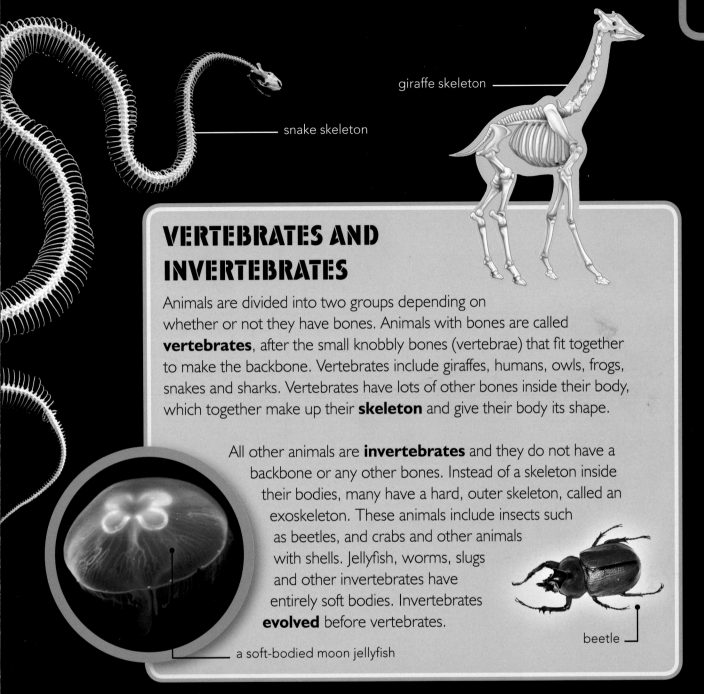

giraffe skeleton

snake skeleton

VERTEBRATES AND INVERTEBRATES

Animals are divided into two groups depending on whether or not they have bones. Animals with bones are called **vertebrates**, after the small knobbly bones (vertebrae) that fit together to make the backbone. Vertebrates include giraffes, humans, owls, frogs, snakes and sharks. Vertebrates have lots of other bones inside their body, which together make up their **skeleton** and give their body its shape.

All other animals are **invertebrates** and they do not have a backbone or any other bones. Instead of a skeleton inside their bodies, many have a hard, outer skeleton, called an exoskeleton. These animals include insects such as beetles, and crabs and other animals with shells. Jellyfish, worms, slugs and other invertebrates have entirely soft bodies. Invertebrates **evolved** before vertebrates.

beetle

a soft-bodied moon jellyfish

SMALLER GROUPS

chimpanzee (ape)

Each large group is divided into smaller groups (or classes), according to the shape and structure of the animals' body and how they live. Vertebrates form five groups – fishes, **amphibians**, **reptiles**, birds and **mammals** – and each of these are subdivided further. Reptiles, for example, are divided into: lizards and snakes, turtles and tortoises, crocodiles and alligators. Each of these is divided into different **species** and families. Boa constrictors, cobras, rattlesnakes and pythons are all different species of snake. Humans are mammals that belong to the group of primates that also includes apes, monkeys and lemurs.

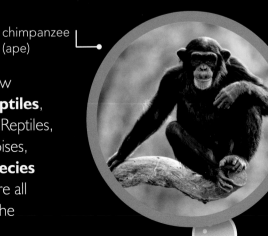

STUDYING HUMANS AND ANIMALS

Scientists carry out research and experiments to help them understand better how the bodies of animals and people work. They look for similarities and differences between different groups and species. They study how human activity and changes in the environment affect animals.

A scientist examines a mouse in the controlled environment of a laboratory.

STRUGGLE TO SURVIVE

Zoologists study animals, both in the wild and in **captivity**. For example, only a small number of giant pandas still live in the wild. Most live in zoos and nature parks but they do not **breed** easily in captivity. Scientists are carrying out research to help more female giant pandas give birth to healthy cubs.

Most giant pandas now live in captivity.

STUDYING HUMANS

Human **biologists** study people. Medical researchers study diseases and their effect on the human body. They try to develop new medicines and medical procedures (operations) and test them on human subjects (many are first tested on animals). Other scientists work to keep people healthy by studying the effects of different diets and types of exercise.

Vaccinations protect us against diseases, such as typhoid.

WORKING SCIENTIFICALLY

In this book, you'll find a range of investigations or experiments that will help you discover how human and animal bodies work.

To do experiments, scientists use careful, logical methods to make sure they get reliable results. The experiments and investigations in this book use four key scientific methods, along with an easy acronym to help you remember them: **ATOM**.

ASK

What do you want to find out?

Asking questions is a really important part of science. Scientists think about what questions they want to answer, and how to do that.

TEST

Setting up an experiment that will test ideas and answer questions

Scientists then design experiments to answer their questions. A test works best if you only test for one thing at a time.

OBSERVE

Key things to look out for

Scientists watch their experiments closely to see what is happening.

MEASURE

Measuring and recording results, such as temperatures, sizes or amounts of time

Making accurate measurements and recording the results shows what the experiment has revealed.

WHAT NEXT?

After each experiment, the 'What next?' section gives you ideas for more activities and experiments, or ways to display your results.

BONES AND CARTILAGE

A vertebrate's skeleton shapes its body and supports its weight. Bones cannot bend and so the bones that form the skeleton link together in joints, which allow the bones to move in different ways.

A dancer moves his legs at the hips. The hip joint is a ball that fits into a **socket**, which allows the hip to **rotate** in different directions.

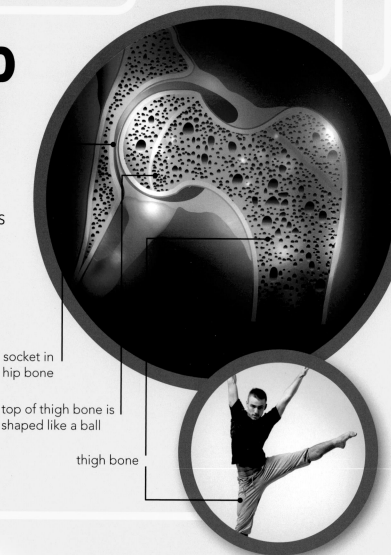

socket in hip bone

top of thigh bone is shaped like a ball

thigh bone

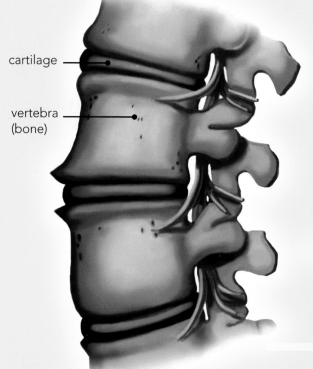

cartilage

vertebra (bone)

CARTILAGE

Bones are strong and hard because they contain the **mineral calcium**. The ends of a bone are covered with **cartilage**. This bendy, rubbery substance cushions the bones as they move. As a bone grows, some of the cartilage at the ends **absorbs** calcium to form new hard bone. Your ears and the tips of your nose and chin contain cartilage, too, but they do not absorb calcium and so remain soft and bendy.

The vertebrae in the backbone are cushioned by pads of cartilage, which stop the bones grinding together.

YOU WILL NEED:

Bones from the wings of
a cooked chicken
2 china or glass bowls
Lemon juice • Vinegar
Measuring jug
Cling film • Paper and pen

SCIENCE EXPERIMENT:

TURNING BONES TO CARTILAGE

You can change a bone back into rubbery cartilage by soaking it in lemon juice or vinegar. The acid dissolves the calcium in the bone.

 ASK

Which liquid will dissolve the calcium in the bone faster?

 **TEST**

- Select and clean the thinnest bone from each chicken wing.
- Measure and pour 100 ml of lemon juice into one of the bowls and 100 ml of vinegar into the other bowl.
- Place a bone in each bowl and cover with cling film.
- Gently test the bones every two days to see if they are bendy.
- Continue to soak each bone until it bends easily.

 OBSERVE

Which liquid begins to work first? Notice which part of the bone softens first. Does any part of the bone not become bendy?

 MEASURE

Make a table to show how long each liquid took to dissolve the calcium in each bone. Was your prediction correct?

WHAT NEXT?

Repeat the experiment with invertebrates that have exoskeletons containing calcium, such as seashells or empty snail shells.

Your voice box (larynx) and **windpipe** (trachea) are made of cartilage. Your larynx opens to make different sounds as you breathe out. Find out how birds and frogs make sounds.

empty snail shell

cartilage

Animal windpipes contain cartilage too. This is a section of a dog's windpipe seen under a microscope.

MOVING ON LAND

Apart from snakes and some amphibians, land vertebrates have legs to move them over the ground. The power to move is produced by **muscles**. They act together with the bones and joints to form **levers** that allow vertebrates to move with less effort.

With their powerful muscles and long legs, the fastest human sprinters cover more than 10 metres a second. At top speed, a cheetah can run three times faster at 30 metres a second.

HOW A LEVER WORKS

A lever magnifies the effect of a force. It does this by turning about a fixed point called the **pivot**. When you stand on tiptoe, the muscles in your calf can **lift** your weight because the force pivots about your toes. Walking involves several muscles, joints and bones that lever you along.

weight —

lever

pivot

Your feet work as levers and pivot around your toes to lift you onto tiptoe.

JUMPING

To jump, you bend your knees and push yourself up and forwards. The muscles store **energy** when you bend and then release it, like a **spring**.

A frog's extra-long back legs give it more spring when it jumps.

LEVER POWER

Flick pellets of paper with different rulers to find out which makes the most effective lever and spring.

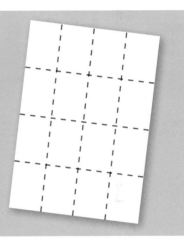

Ask

Which ruler will propel pellets of paper farthest?

Test

- Fold the paper in half four times.
- Unfold the paper and cut along the folds to give 16 equal pieces.
- Scrunch up each piece to make a pellet.
- Mark a chalk line in an empty space on the floor.
- Place the first ruler upright on the line and hold a pellet at the top end.
- Hold the bottom of the ruler firmly on the line and bend back the top with the pellet. Take your top hand away, releasing the pellet.
- Repeat three times with each ruler.

Observe

Which ruler propels the pellets farthest, and which propels them highest? Does extra height help the pellet to travel farther?

Measure

Measure the distance from the ruler to where each pellet lands. Work out the average distance for each ruler.

WHAT NEXT?

Make a bar chart of your results. Next try the experiment again, but this time move the pivot (your hand) further up the ruler. What difference does this make to the distance the paper pellets fly?

Here the hand (pivot) is at the bottom of the ruler and the ruler bends easily. Moving the pivot up the ruler should make the ruler harder to bend.

YOU WILL NEED:

3 rulers of different lengths and bendiness
Sheet of A4 paper
Scissors • Chalk
Measuring tape
Paper and pen

BUILT TO FLY

Bats, most birds and some insects can fly, not just because they have wings but also because their bodies are lightweight.

STRONG ENOUGH?

Birds have hollow bones. Although this makes them lightweight, a bird's wings also have to be strong to produce enough force to fly, often against strong winds. What makes hollow bones so strong?

A dragonfly's wings are so thin, you can see through them.

This cross-section of a bird's bone shows that the hollow space is criss-crossed with supporting pieces of bone.

LIGHTWEIGHT WINGS

Insects' wings, such as those of the dragonfly, are made of fine **gossamer**. Bats' wings consist of thin skin stretched between their long 'finger' bones. Birds' wings are made of slender bones and feathers, which are hollow to make them even lighter.

bat

The large, flat surface **area** of a wing gives animals, such as this bird, lift, which allows them to fly.

SCIENCE EXPERIMENT:

HOLLOW SHAPES

Compare the strength of different hollow shapes by making models from paper. Test round, square and triangular tubes.

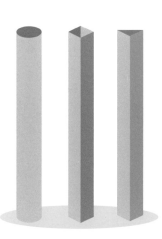

Ask

Which shape of hollow tube will support the greatest weight?

Test

- Make each tube by first folding a sheet of A4 paper in half lengthwise. Then roll or fold along the long sides.
- Make a round tube by rolling the folded paper lengthwise so the sides just meet. Join the long sides together with sticky tape.
- Make a square tube by folding the folded sheet into quarters. Join the open long sides together with sticky tape.
- Make a triangular tube by folding the folded sheet into equal thirds. Join the open long sides together with sticky tape.
- Stand the first tube on one end. Balance a can on top of it. You may have to steady the tube with your hand. Keep adding cans until the tube collapses.
- Repeat the experiment with the other tubes.

Observe

Note how many cans each tube can support before collapsing.

Measure

Make a table to compare the result for each tube. Find out the **formulas** for calculating the area of a circle, a square and a triangle and use them to compare the area of the end of each tube.

WHAT NEXT?

Make three new tubes and pack each one with sheets of kitchen roll. Repeat the experiment to compare the strength of a solid tube with the hollow one.

SUPER STREAMLINED

Animals that move fast through the air, on land or in the water have one thing in common – their bodies are **streamlined**. This means that they are shaped so that air or water flows smoothly around them, allowing them to cut easily through the air or water.

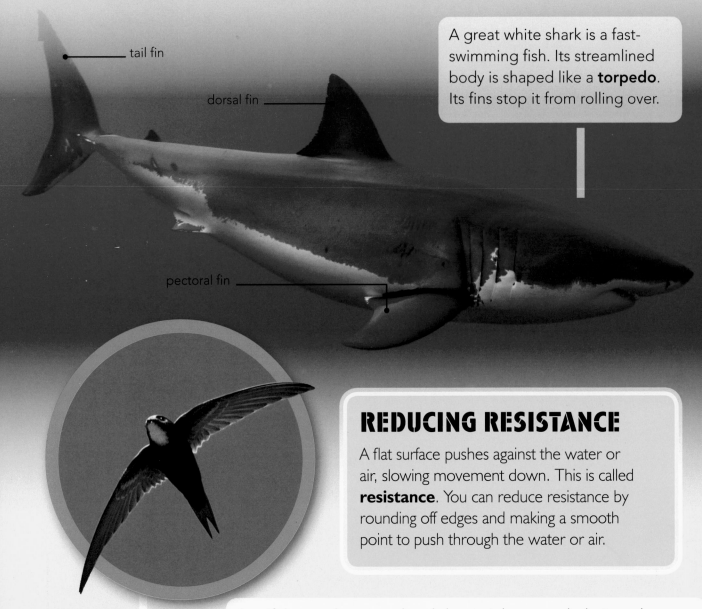

tail fin

dorsal fin

pectoral fin

A great white shark is a fast-swimming fish. Its streamlined body is shaped like a **torpedo**. Its fins stop it from rolling over.

REDUCING RESISTANCE

A flat surface pushes against the water or air, slowing movement down. This is called **resistance**. You can reduce resistance by rounding off edges and making a smooth point to push through the water or air.

A swift has a very streamlined shape. It has rounded wings that slice through the air, a torpedo-shaped body and a pointed head.

YOU WILL NEED:

3 strips of modelling clay
Enough gelatine to make
570 ml of jelly • Hot water
Measuring jug • Fork
Scissors • Timer
A 1.5-litre plastic bottle with
the top cut off
Notebook and pen

SCIENCE EXPERIMENT:

FALLING THROUGH JELLY

Compare which shape is the most streamlined by timing how long each takes to fall through liquid. Falling through liquid jelly is like falling in slow motion because a thicker liquid offers more resistance to the shapes falling through it.

Ask an adult to
help you make the jelly.

 ASK

Which shape will fall fastest through the jelly?
Which will fall the slowest?

modelling
clay

 TEST

- Make a sphere, a cube and a torpedo shape from modelling clay, using one strip for each.
- Ask an adult to make the jelly in the measuring jug and leave it in the fridge to set.
- When the jelly has set, stir it with a fork to break it up into small pieces.
- Gently mix in hot water, drop by drop, until the jelly is just liquid enough to allow the shapes to fall through it.
- Pour the jelly fluid into the plastic bottle.
- Place the three shapes gently on the surface of the jelly.

 OBSERVE

Watch the shapes as they fall through the jelly.

WHAT NEXT?

Take the fastest shape and see if you can improve the design by adding fins to make it even faster.

 MEASURE

Time how long it takes for each shape to fall to the bottom of the jug. Were your predictions correct?

Engineers copy the streamlined shapes of animals when they design fast vehicles, such as this fighter jet. Can you see shark-like fins on this jet?

15

SHARP SIGHT

All vertebrates have two eyes, but the position of the eyes is different for **predators** and **prey**. Most predators have eyes on the front of their head, while prey animals have eyes on the sides.

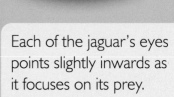

JUDGING DISTANCE

A predator, such as a cat, often creeps up on its prey before pouncing. Each eye faces forwards and sees the prey from a slightly different angle. This creates overlapping views, which help a predator to tell exactly how far away its prey is. Being able to judge distances accurately is vital to its survival.

Each of the jaguar's eyes points slightly inwards as it focuses on its prey.

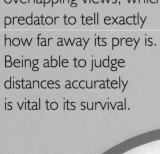

A rabbit is a prey animal. It can keep watch for predators almost all around it without having to turn its head from side to side.

KEEPING WATCH

A prey animal is more likely to survive if it can spot a predator before it gets too close. Having an eye on each side of its head allows it to scan a much wider area and, by feeding together in groups, they keep watch in every direction.

SCIENCE EXPERIMENT:

SEE FOR YOURSELF!

Try this paper clip test with a friend to see whether two forward-facing eyes are better at judging distances than one eye.

Ask

Will two eyes judge distance better than one eye?

Human eyes face forwards because people are predators not prey.

Test

- Sit opposite your friend at a table. Ask your friend to cover one eye with the patch. Put the cup about 60 cm in front of your friend.
- Hold a paper clip about 40 cm above the table. Move the paper clip slowly in front, behind and over the cup.
- Tell your friend to say 'now' when they think the paper clip is over the cup. Drop the paper clip when they say 'now'. Repeat with four more paper clips.
- Remove the eye patch and repeat the test.

Observe

Does your friend get better at judging where the cup is? Are they more successful when using both eyes?

Measure

If the paper clip misses the cup, measure how far it falls from it. Make a table to compare the results for using one eye with those for using both eyes.

WHAT NEXT?

Repeat the experiment, first with the cup closer to your friend and then farther away. Does changing the distance change the result?

Most animals have eyes that either always face forwards or always face sideways. A few animals have extraordinary eyes. Find out what a chameleon can do with its eyes.

chameleon

LOCATING SOUND

Many animals have a better sense of hearing than we do. For example, cats, rabbits and zebra have large ears that prick up to collect more **sound waves**. In addition, they can swivel their ears towards the direction of the sound.

Zebras prick up their ears to listen out for the rustle of danger.

ECHOLOCATION

Bats and dolphins use **echolocation** to help them 'see' in the dark or in murky water. They emit (produce) squeaks that are too high-pitched for other animals to hear. As the squeaks echo (bounce) back from nearby surfaces, the animal forms a picture of what is around it.

Tiger moths emit clicks to protect themselves from being hunted by bats. The moths' clicks confuse the bats' echolocation!

A dolphin uses echolocation to help it hunt for prey.

THE BAT TEST

How well can you locate the direction a sound comes from?

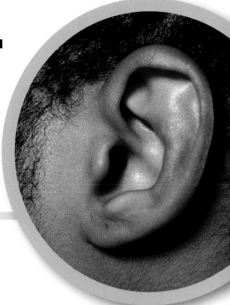

 ASK

Will it be easier to pinpoint sounds in front, behind or at the side of the head?

> A human ear is fixed in place on the side of the head. It can't swivel to locate sound.

 TEST

- Chalk a cross in the middle of a large space.
- Fold a string in half and hold the centre on the cross.
- Ask two people to pull the ends of the string into a straight line across the cross and stand on their end.
- Repeat with the other strings so you end up with eight people standing in a circle as shown in the diagram.
- Blindfold the ninth person and stand them at the centre, facing a particular direction (front).
- The tenth person points to someone in the circle, who claps once.
- The blindfolded person points to where they heard the sound.
- The tenth person places a marker near the edge of the circle in the direction the blindfolded person pointed.
- Repeat the experiment, choosing which person should clap in a random order. When everyone has clapped, swap the person who is blindfolded.

 OBSERVE

Who is most successful at detecting the direction of sound? Who would make the best bat?

 MEASURE

For each person tested, record the distance between each marker and the person who actually clapped. Who is most accurate?

WHAT NEXT?

Draw a large circle on paper divided into sectors, like the strings. Plot all the guesses onto the circle. Are the guesses to the front and back of the head more, or less, accurate than those to the sides?

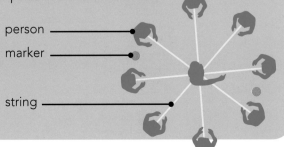

person ————

marker ————

string ————

INTERESTING SMELLS

Many animals rely on their sense of smell to find food and a mate and to recognise each other. Dogs and sharks have a particularly good sense of smell. Insects, such as bees and butterflies, can detect smells many kilometres away.

Honeybees and other insects use their **antennae** to detect smell.

antenna

Dogs have 40 times as many smell **receptors** as humans. A Labrador's sense of smell is so good that Labradors are often trained by the police to detect drugs and explosives.

TASTE AND SMELL

Smell is important to humans too. Some smells warn of danger. Food that smells bad may be rotten and dangerous to eat. When food smells good, however, we want to eat it. Smell receptors are in the nose and taste receptors are in the mouth. The sense of taste combines with the sense of smell to give a stronger taste.

When chemicals from an object reach the taste or smell receptors, the receptors send information to the brain.

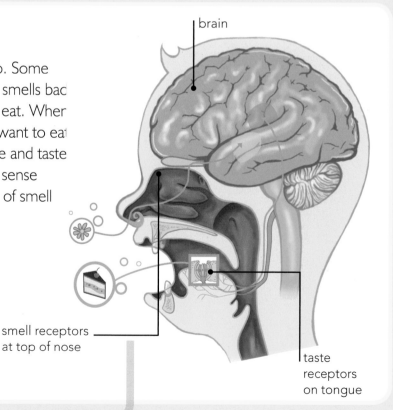

brain

smell receptors at top of nose

taste receptors on tongue

YOU WILL NEED:

A friend
An apple, a crisp pear
and a raw potato
Peeler • Knife
Fork • Blindfold
Drink of water
Notepad and pen

SCIENCE EXPERIMENT:

TASTE OR SMELL?

**How well can you identify tastes when
your nose is blocked?**

Ask an adult to
supervise you when
using the knife.

 ASK

Will tasting something with your nose blocked make telling
one taste from another easier, harder or just the same?

 TEST

- Peel and slice the apple into about 8 pieces. Repeat with the pear and
  potato, making all the pieces roughly the same size and shape.
- Blindfold your friend and ask them to squeeze their nostrils tight shut.
- Spear a slice of apple with the fork and give it to your friend to identify the
  taste. Ask them to place it on their tongue and hold it there for 30 seconds
  before they chew it. Repeat with a slice of pear, then a slice of potato. Give
  your friend a drink of water to clean their mouth between each test.
- Keeping the blindfold on, tell your friend to release their nostrils.
  Then repeat the test.

 OBSERVE

Make a note of each type of slice and whether your
friend identified it correctly with and without their nostrils
blocked. Is any type of slice easier or harder to identify?

WHAT NEXT?

Change places
with your friend
and repeat the
experiment.

 MEASURE

Make a table or chart of your results.

This illustration shows human
taste receptors – called papillae –
magnified many times. There are
taste buds inside each papilla.

TEETH AND BEAKS

Many animals crunch up food before they swallow it. Their teeth or beaks show the type of food they eat.

Carnivores (meat-eaters) have **fangs** and sharp teeth. Herbivores (plant-eaters), such as sheep and cows, have mainly flat teeth for chewing plants. Omnivores, such as humans, have a mixture of sharp and flat teeth as they eat both meat and plants.

A crocodile uses its many sharp teeth to catch, grip and tear flesh from its prey.

A sheep has flat front teeth only in the lower jaw. It has a hard pad in the upper jaw.

zebra finch

BIRDS' BEAKS

Birds do not have teeth but their beaks are shaped to suit the type of food they eat. Seed-eaters, such as the zebra finch, have short stubby beaks, for example.

THE COLOUR OF FOOD

Food looks appetising when it is the right colour and smells good, but would you eat green eggs? We avoid food that is the wrong colour, because it may be unfit to eat.

SCIENCE EXPERIMENT:
COLOURING BIRD FOOD

Are birds, like humans, affected by the colour of food? This experiment will work best in winter, when the birds are short of food.

YOU WILL NEED:

White rice
Red, blue and green food dyes
2 large oranges • Knife
Kebab skewer
4 pieces of 70-cm-long string
Kitchen scales
Tablespoon • Small saucepan
Notepad and paper

 ## Ask

Will birds prefer a particular colour of food?

 ## Test

- Cut the oranges in half and scoop out the fruit to make four orange cups.
- With the skewer, make two holes on opposite sides of each cup, about 1 cm below the rim. Thread a piece of string through the holes and knot securely.
- Make small holes in the bottom for drainage.

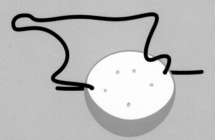

- Measure 1 tablespoon of rice and 2–3 tablespoons of water into a pan and simmer until the water is absorbed. This gives you a portion of white rice.
- Cook three more portions, adding a few drops of a different food dye to each of these three portions.
- When each portion of rice has cooled, spoon it into an orange cup.
- Weigh the cups and then hang them from the branch of a tree.

This great tit knows that a sunflower seed is good to eat.

 ## Observe

Watch the cups from a distance. Try to spot which cup the birds like best.

 ## Measure

Weigh the cups again after a week. The cup that loses most weight contains the birds' favourite coloured rice.

WHAT NEXT?

Make a bar chart to show the results.

Find out about birds that eat meat, such as vultures and crows. What would humans find off-putting about the food these birds eat?

23

BREATHING

All animals need to take in **oxygen** to survive. Like all mammals, air passes from your mouth or through your nostrils and nose into air tubes that lead to your lungs.

nostril

BREATHE IN

When you breathe in, your lungs expand and the ribs move outwards. When you breathe out, your lungs become smaller and the ribs move in.

Mammals, such as this hippo, have two nostrils through which they breathe air into their nose.

HOW LUNGS WORK

The **diaphragm** is a flat sheet of muscle that controls breathing. When the diaphragm tightens and moves down, your lungs pull in air to fill the space. When the diaphragm relaxes and moves up, air is pushed out (see page 25).

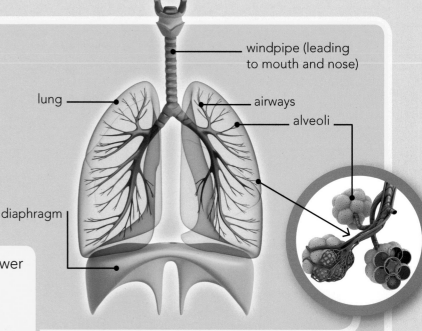

windpipe (leading to mouth and nose)

lung

airways

alveoli

diaphragm

Your airways branch into narrower and narrower tubes that each end in a tiny balloon-like sac, which is called an alveoli.

GILLS

Most fish don't have lungs and can't breathe in air. They take in oxygen from the water through organs called gills. As water passes over the gills, oxygen is absorbed into their blood.

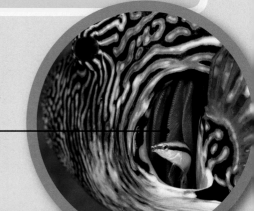

gills

YOU WILL NEED:

A 1-litre empty plastic bottle
A disposable vinyl glove
Strong sticky tape, such as gaffer tape • Scissors
A bendy drinking straw
Modelling clay
A tumbler of water
Food colouring
Small plastic ruler

SCIENCE EXPERIMENT:

MAKE A MODEL LUNG

This experiment shows how air (or in this case water) is pulled into the lungs when the diaphragm moves down.

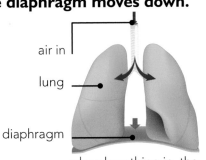
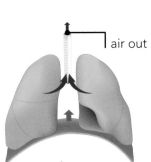

air in

lung

diaphragm

air out

when breathing in, the diaphragm moves down

when breathing out, the diaphragm moves up

Ask

Will the model lung suck up water?

Test

- Ask an adult to cut off the bottom of the bottle.
- Stretch the glove over the open base of the bottle and secure it with sticky tape.
- Gather the rest of the glove together and knot it so that it forms a tight surface across the base.
- Wrap the modelling clay around the short end of the straw and push it into the neck of the bottle. Mould the clay to form an airtight seal.
- Add a few drops of colouring to the tumbler of water.
- Fix the ruler against the long end of the straw with the sticky tape.
- Put the end of the ruler and straw in the tumbler of water.

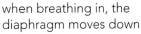

Observe

What happens when you gently pull the knotted end of the glove?

Measure

Hold the straw and ruler in the water so that the surface is at the zero mark on the ruler. Pull the glove and measure how far the water moves up the straw. Repeat, pulling the glove farther each time.

WHAT NEXT?

Remove the tumbler of water and blow through the straw into the bottle. What happens to the glove?

Find out about how insects and other invertebrates get oxygen into their bodies.

UNIQUE INDIVIDUALS

Scientists classify living things according to what they have in common, but humans and other animals tell each other apart by the things that are different. We may recognise the shape of a face, the colour of someone's hair, and the sound of a voice. Many animals recognise each other's distinct smell.

Many types of animals have unique skin patterns. No two zebras have exactly the same pattern of stripes.

UNIQUE PATTERNS

With humans, identical twins are difficult to tell apart, but even identical twins have unique patterns in their irises and fingerprints. A fingerprint is made by the small ridges in the skin under the ends of your fingers. When you touch something smooth or pick it up, you leave an imprint of your fingertips on the object.

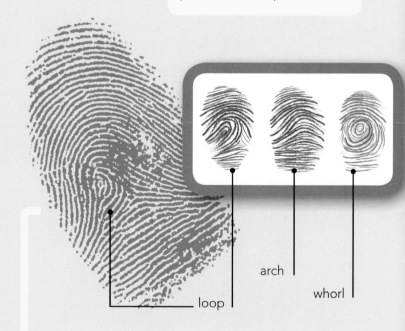

arch

whorl

loop

every iris has a unique pattern

The three main fingerprint patterns are loop, arch and whorl. Some fingerprints are a combination of the main patterns.

When the police arrest a suspect, they record their fingerprints to see if they match any found at the scene of a crime.

YOU WILL NEED:

Charcoal
Several sheets of white paper
Sticky tape
Magnifying glass
Notepad and pen

SCIENCE EXPERIMENT:

IDENTIFYING FINGERPRINTS

Use charcoal and white paper to compare your fingerprints with those of your friends and family.

 ASK

Do members of the same family have similar fingerprints?

 OBSERVE

Check each print as you make it. If it is not clear, then do it again.

 MEASURE

Make a chart to compare the prints on each hand. Note whether it is a whorl, loop or arch or a combination of these features. Use the magnifying glass to help you count the number of whorls, loops and arches. Are any sets of prints similar? Whose set of prints are the most different from your own?

TEST

- Rub a stick of charcoal over an area of paper larger than the end of your thumb.
- Press the end of your right thumb onto the charcoal.
- Place a piece of sticky tape over the charcoal on your thumb.
- Carefully remove the tape and stick it onto a clean sheet of paper. Label the print 'thumb'.
- Repeat with the rest of the fingers on your right hand.
- Take the fingerprints on the right hand of a friend and of a close member of your family.

WHAT NEXT?

Take the prints from people's left hands and compare them.

A detective tests for fingerprints on a tumbler by lightly dusting powder over the surface of the glass.

My right hand

thumb   finger 1   finger 2   finger 3   finger 4

READING YOUR RESULTS

When scientists do experiments, they get results. Even if nothing happened as they expected, that is a result too! All results can be useful, but it is important to understand them. Here are some guidelines that scientists use to learn from their results.

USE A CONTROL

In the Colouring Bird Food experiment on page 23, the 'control' is the cup with undyed white rice. A control is a normal version of the set-up, without the things that are being tested – in this case different colours of dyed rice.

It's really important that, apart from the thing being tested, the control version matches the test versions in every way. So you use the same amount of the same type of food. Then you know that any differences in your results are purely down to the colour of the rice.

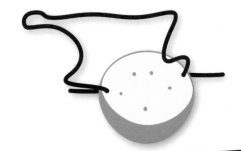

REPEAT AND VERIFY

An experiment may work well once, but what if that was a fluke? So that they can be sure of their results, scientists often repeat an experiment several times.

CHECK FOR BIAS

If you're *really* hoping for an exciting result, it's possible you might accidentally-on-purpose 'help' your experiment along by ignoring something that doesn't fit with what you wanted. This is called 'bias' and can happen without you even realising it.

OUTLIERS

What if you were conducting the Falling Through Jelly experiment on page 15 and found that the cube fell faster than the other shapes?

You'd probably be surprised, because the cube has flat sides and so should produce more resistance as it falls. This unusual result is called an outlier and scientists have to check outliers carefully and work out why they have happened. Perhaps the cube was made with a bigger strip of modelling clay and was heavier than the others.

KEEPING RECORDS

Writing down the details of each experiment and what the results were is essential for scientists. Not only does it help to explain their work to others; it also means they can use results to look for patterns. For example, in the Turning Bones to Cartilage experiment on page 9, does the thickness of a bone or shell affect the result?

MAKING MISTAKES

If you spot a mistake, start the experiment again. It would be an even bigger mistake to use the results from a badly run experiment.

However, if a mistake makes something interesting happen, you could set up a new experiment to test for that instead. Many important discoveries have been made this way. For example, in 1895 Wilhelm Röntgen (1845–1923) was investigating cathode rays when he noticed an eerie picture of the bones in his own hand on the screen. He called them X-rays because he did not know what they were.

GLOSSARY

absorb To take in or soak up.

acid A substance that turns universal indicator paper red.

amphibian A vertebrate that usually breathes through gills as young and into lungs when adult.

antennae Long, thin feelers that some animals, such as bees, use to smell and touch.

area A measurement of the amount of space on a surface.

biologist A scientist who studies life and living things.

breed When animals mate and produce animal offspring.

calcium A substance contained in some foods that is used to strengthen hard parts of a body, such as bones, teeth and shells.

captivity To be held in an enclosure or cage; not in the wild.

cartilage A rubbery substance found at the ends of bones. Cartilage forms new bone when it absorbs calcium.

diaphragm A flat sheet of muscle that is situated below the lungs and controls breathing.

dissolve When a solid mixes with a liquid and becomes part of the liquid.

echolocation A way of detecting where something is by making sounds and 'reading' their echoes.

energy The ability to make something move or happen.

environment The place an animal lives in.

evolve To develop gradually over a long period of time.

fangs Long, sharp teeth.

formula A group of symbols that show how to calculate something mathematically.

gossamer Very thin fabric or thread, such as that woven by spiders.

invertebrates Animals that do not have a backbone or any other bones.

lever A simple machine that has the effect of changing a small force into a large force.

life processes The seven activities – movement, nutrition, senses, respiration, excretion, growth and reproduction – which identify whether something is a living thing.

lift An upward force.

mammal A vertebrate that breathes air, has hair and drinks its mother's milk when it is young.

mineral A natural substance found in the Earth that is pure or the same all the way through, and is not a mixture of things.

muscle Part of the body that helps produce movement.

oxygen A gas that all animals need to take in to survive.

pivot To turn about a point.

predator An animal that hunts other animals for food.

prey An animal that is hunted by another animal for food.

receptors Parts of the nervous system that react to particular things in the environment. For example, taste receptors react to chemicals dissolved in saliva.

reptile A vertebrate that usually has dry, scaly skin.

resistance Pushing back against a force.

rotate To turn in a circle around an axis.

skeleton All the bones in a body. The skeleton provides a frame that gives the body its shape and supports the vital organs, such as the heart.

socket A hollow shape into which something else fits.

sound wave The vibration of sound as it travels through the air, a liquid or other object.

species The scientific name for a particular type of living thing.

spring A simple machine that is squashed to store energy and then regains its shape when it releases the energy.

streamlined Shaped so that an object can move smoothly and easily through air or a liquid.

torpedo A long, streamlined weapon, designed to use in water.

vertebrate An animal that has a backbone and other bones.

windpipe The flexible pipe that goes from the throat to the lungs.

zoologist A scientist who studies animals.

BOOKS

Bodyworks (series) by Thomas Canavan,
Franklin Watts

Moving Up with Science: The Body
by Peter Riley, Franklin Watts

Speedy Science by Angela Royston (ed),
Franklin Watts

The Story of You by Anna Claybourne,
Wayland

Your Brilliant Body (series) by
Paul Mason, Wayland

Other books in this series:
Science Skills Sorted: Plants
Science Skills Sorted: Habitats
Science Skills Sorted: Life Cycles
Science Skills Sorted: Evolution
and Classification
Science Skills Sorted: Rocks
and Fossils

WEBSITES

https://www.rspb.org.uk/makeahomeforwildlife/advice/helpingbirds/feeding/whatfood/
This section of the Royal Society for the Protection of Birds (RSPB) gives advice on suitable food for feeding wild birds and provides a guide to help you identify some of the birds that might visit your bird feeder.

https://www.brainpop.com/science/scientificinquiry/scientificmethod/
Watch the video to see Tim and Moby put scientific method into action to solve a problem.

http://kidshealth.org/en/kids/experiment-main.html
Try the experiments on this website to test your senses.
You can choose from more than one for each sense.

http://www.oum.ox.ac.uk/thezone/animals/life/
Oxford University's Museum of Natural History has created this website to explain the seven life processes shared by all living things. Do the quiz at the end to test your knowledge.

http://www.kidzone.ws/animals/animal_classes.htm
This website gives a clear description of the main classes (groups) of vertebrates and of a large group of invertebrates called arthropods, which includes insects, spiders, crabs and many more.

INDEX

SCIENCE SKILLS SORTED
These are the lists of contents for the titles in the Science Skills Sorted series:

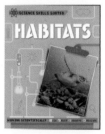

PLANTS

What makes a plant a plant? • The science of plants • Working scientifically • Seeds • Plant defence • What plants need to grow • Surviving a drought • Water content • How leaves work • Helping nature • Flowers and seeds • Autumn colours • Cloning plants • Reading your results • Glossary and further information • Index

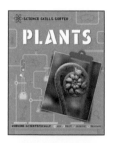

HABITATS

What is a habitat? • The science of habitats • Working scientifically • Wildlife habitats • Adaptations • Moving in • Blending in • Extreme habitats • Keystone species • How trees help • Balancing the numbers • Building the environment • Climate change • Reading your results • Glossary and further information • Index

LIFE CYCLES

What is a life cycle? • The science of life cycles • Working scientifically • From seed to seed • Eggs and babies • Metamorphosis • Finding a mate • Dividing bacteria • Budding yeast • Spreading out • Generations • Life cycle maths • Hitching a ride • Reading your results • Glossary and further information • Index

EVOLUTION AND CLASSIFICATION

What is evolution? • The science of evolution • Working scientifically • Evolution in action • Survival of the fittest • Finding food • Adapting to habitats • Winning a mate • Genes and genetic traits • Classification • Sorting it out • Body plans • The DNA key • Reading your results • Glossary and further information • Index

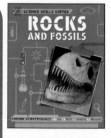

ROCKS AND FOSSILS

What are rocks, minerals and fossils? • The science of rocks and fossils• Working scientifically • Types of rock • Rocks and water • Minerals and crystals • How hard? • Weathering and erosion • Expanding ice • Making mountains • Volcanoes and earthquakes • How fossils form • Fossil puzzles • Reading your results • Glossary and further information • Index

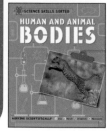

HUMAN AND ANIMAL BODIES

Humans and other animals? • Studying humans and animals• Working scientifically • Bones • Moving on land • Built to fly • Super streamlined • Sharp sight • Locating sound • Interesting smell • Teeth and beaks • Breathing • Unique individuals • Reading your results • Glossary and further information • Index